discovering Shakespeare

Wilfried Brusch

Ernst Klett Verlag
Stuttgart München Düsseldorf Leipzig

Discovering Shakespeare

compiled and edited by Professor Dr. Wilfried Brusch, Hamburg

Acknowledgements

The editors wish to thank all authors, publishers and literary agencies who have given permission to use copyright material. Sources are given underneath all the texts. The following list acknowledges copyright holders who are not identical with the publishers quoted and includes additional specifications demanded by copyright holders.

P. 13: © Penguin Books; pp. 28–31: © Methuen, reprinted by permission of Reed Books; pp. 32–35: copyright © 1942 James Thurber. Copyright © 1970 Rosemary A. Thurber; pp. 36–37: © Hutchinson; p. 38: reprinted by permission of the publisher; pp. 39–40: reprinted by permission of Blackwell Publishers; pp. 41–42: excerpt from BABBIT by Sinclair Lewis, copyright 1922 by Harcourt Brace & Company and renewed 1950 Sinclair Lewis, reprinted by permission of the publisher; p. 43: reprinted by permission of Max Reinhardt, Reinhardt Books Ltd; pp. 44–45: reprinted by permission of the *Deutsche Shakespeare-Gesellschaft;* p. 46a): reprinted by permission of Jarrold Publishing; p. 46b): *The Observer* ©; pp. 47–48: © *The Guardian.*

Picture credits

Archiv für Kunst und Geschichte, Berlin: p. 40; Clive Barda/Performing Arts Library: p. 44; © BBC, London: p. 45; Bridgeman Art Library, London: pp. 7b (National Maritime Museum, London), 13 (Hatfield House, Hertfordshire), 21 (Boughton House, Northamptonshire), 27 (Woburn Abbey, Bedfordshire); Gareth and Barbara Lloyd Evans, Everyman's Companion to Shakespeare, J.M. Dent & Sons, London,1978: p. 8b; by permission of the Folger Shakespeare Library, Washington, D.C.: p. 7a; Guildhall Library, Corporation of London: p. 8a; Glenine Hamlyn, Stuttgart: pp. 20, 22; Hulton Deutsch Collection Ltd, London: p. 9; Kinoarchiv Engelmeier, Hamburg: pp. 17, 25, 31, 39, 42a; Kobal Collection, London: pp. 23 (Robert Penn), 30; Richard Kralina/The International Shakespeare Globe Centre Ltd., London: p. 15; Mansell Collection Ltd, London: p. 12; © 1994 Ken Reynolds/ Barbican Centre: p. 48; The Shakespeare Birthplace Trust, Stratford-upon-Avon: pp. 29, 35, 38, 42b; Stratford-upon-Avon & District Marketing Limited, Stratford-upon-Avon: p. 5b; © The Sunday Times, London 1995: p. 11; TCL/Bavaria, Munich: p. 19; Monika Türk, Stuttgart: p. 47.

Every effort has been made to trace owners of copyright material, but in some cases this has not proved possible and repeated enquiries have remained unanswered. The publishers would be glad to hear from any further copyright owners of material reproduced in this book.

First edition 1 8 7 | 2004 03 02

The last figure shown denotes the year of impression. All printings of this edition are identical.

Editor: Glenine Hamlyn, M.A.

Cover illustration: detail from Cornelis Visscher, *Long View of London* (1616), copyright British Museum, London; Shakespeare portrait: Katharina Weinreich, Stuttgart.

Printed in Germany

ISBN 3-12-576350-9

Contents

1 The Seven Ages of Man

Do you ever think about where have you come from and where you are going in life? In Shakespeare's day – as in every age – artists, writers, and ordinary people asked this question. They divided life into seven phases. Before you read Shakespeare's words on the subject, think about the phases you might divide life into. How many are there? Write a short, humorous description of each phase, then exchange descriptions with your neighbour and compare them.

All the world's a stage,
And all the men and women merely players:
They have their exits and their entrances;
And one man in his time plays many parts,
His acts being seven ages. At first the infant,
Mewling and puking in the nurse's arms.
Then the whining schoolboy, with his satchel,
And shining morning face, creeping like snail
Unwillingly to school. And then the lover,
Sighing like furnace, with a woeful ballad
Made to his mistress' eyebrow. Then a soldier,
Full of strange oaths, and bearded like the pard,
Jealous in honour, sudden and quick in quarrel,
Seeking the bubble reputation
Even in the cannon's mouth. And then the justice,
In fair round belly with good capon lin'd,
With eyes severe, and beard of formal cut,
Full of wise saws and modern instances;
And so he plays his part. The sixth age shifts
Into the lean and slipper'd pantaloon,
With spectacles on nose and pouch on side,
His youthful hose, well sav'd, a world too wide
For his shrunk shank: and his big manly voice,
Turning again toward childish treble, pipes
And whistles in his sound. Last scene of all,
That ends this strange eventful history,
Is second childishness and mere oblivion,
Sans teeth, sans eyes, sans taste, sans everything.

As You Like It *Act II Scene 7 ll. 139–166*

6 **to mewl** to cry weakly
6 **to puke** to lose food and drink through the mouth after eating *(vulgar in modern English)*
7 **to whine** to complain
7 **satchel** school bag
10 **furnace** ['--] large, very hot oven
10 **woeful** sad
12 **oath** *here:* swearword
12 **pard** *(old use)* leopard, panther
13 **jealous** ['dʒeləs] *here:* very enthusiastic
14 **to seek** *(old use)* to look for
14 **bubble** *here: s.th.* shortlived
15 **justice** *here:* judge
16 **capon** ['keɪpən] male chicken fattened for food
16 **to line** *here:* to fill
17 **severe** [sə'vɪə] very serious
18 **saw** *here:* a short, well-known saying
18 **instance** example
20 **lean** thin
20 **pantaloon** funny old man, character in a comedy
21 **pouch** small soft leather bag
22 **hose** tight-fitting leg coverings worn by men in Shakespeare's day
23 **to shrink** to grow smaller
23 **shank** *(old use)* leg from knee to ankle
24 **treble** *here:* high-pitched sound
27 **mere** only
27 **oblivion** *here:* loss of memory
28 **sans** [sænz] *(old use, French)* without

A closer look

1. The seven ages of man according to Shakespeare: list them and describe each one briefly.
2. The illustration on the opposite page is from the 15th century. What is the general idea? Describe the figures in detail.
3. Compare Shakespeare's text with the illustration. Are their messages identical, or are there differences?
4. Now compare your description of the phases of life with Shakespeare's and discuss the differences.

In your opinion

"All the world's a stage". Is life really like a theatre performance? List similarities and differences between life and the theatre, then discuss these or write a short essay on the topic.

A fifteenth-century illustration from Archaeologia *(1853) showing the progression from Generatio (Birth) to Corruptio (Death).*

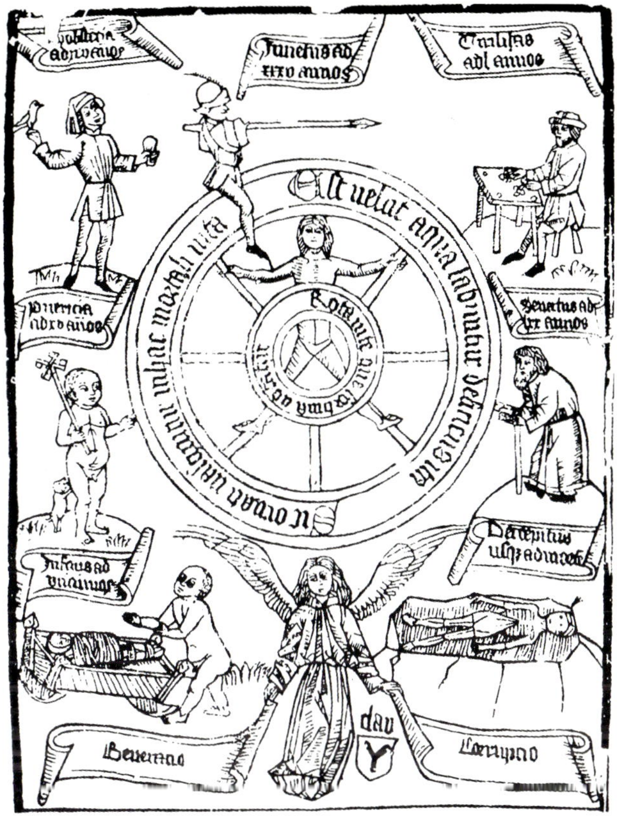

2 Who Was William Shakespeare?

Considering that Shakespeare is generally regarded to be the greatest writer in the English language, it is surprising that relatively little is known of his life. Undoubtedly the political, social and cultural conditions in England at the time played a role in Shakespeare's career, so they help us to complete the picture.

By modern standards Shakespeare did not live long at all – he died at the age of 52.

Before you look at details of Shakespeare's life (on the next page), note down all you know about world events in the late 1400s and 1500s. What cultural movements were important? What discoveries did Europeans make? What political events were important for England? Do you know anything about social conditions at the time?

Shakespeare's birthplace

The life and times of Shakespeare

1564 William Shakespeare baptized on April 26 in Stratford-upon-Avon, Warwickshire.
Shakespeare would have attended a grammar school and learnt Latin and Greek.

1582 Shakespeare marries Anne Hathaway, a local woman eight years his senior.

1583 Birth of Shakespeare's daughter Susanna.

1584 Shakespeare a rising playwright in London.

1585 Birth of the twins Hamnet and Judith.

1592 Shakespeare joins *The Lord Chamberlain's Men*, London's leading theatre group.

1597 Shakespeare purchases "New Place", a large house in Stratford-upon-Avon.

1599 Opening of Globe Theatre, Bankside, built partly with wood from "The Theatre".
The Lord Chamberlain's Men become *The King's Men* with the support of the King.

1608 Birth of Elizabeth Hall, Shakespeare's granddaughter.

1609 First edition of Shakespeare's *Sonnets* printed.

1610 Shakespeare retires to "New Place".

1613 The Globe Theatre destroyed by fire.

1616 Death of Shakespeare on 23 April.

1623 First Folio edition of Shakespeare's plays published.

1558 Elizabeth I crowned Queen of England.
The new queen was highly educated in the Greek and Roman classics and encouraged culture and learning.

1576 London's first theatre, "The Theatre", opened outside the north-east city walls.
Plays were often performed previously – for the masses – in inn-yards.
In keeping with the Renaissance, drama was no longer limited to the enactment of Biblical stories. Morality plays (plays in which the characters represented clear moral values) became popular.
Dramatists such as Christopher Marlowe, a contemporary of Shakespeare, wrote imitations of classical Greek plays and began treating historical subjects.
The Elizabethan Age was also an age of music.

1588 Defeat of the Spanish Armada.
England enjoys wealth and freedom from outside threat.

1603 Death of Queen Elizabeth I and accession of King James I.

1607 First English settlement in Jamestown, Virginia.

1618 Beginning of the Thirty Years' War on the continent.

to baptize to place water on a child's head in a ceremony as a sign that the child is part of the church
grammar school school open to all boys in Shakespeare's day, teaching Latin, Greek and other subjects ...
inn guesthouse for travellers
accession act of becoming the ruler of a country

A closer look
1. Name some of the main historical and cultural features of the Elizabethan Age.
2. In what way did conditions in Shakespeare's day provide favourable conditions for the development of drama?

The portrait of Shakespeare by Droeshout, reproduced on the title page of the First Folio edition of Shakespeare's plays.

A painting of 1588 (English school, 16th century), showing English ships and the Spanish Armada.

3 Entertainment in Shakespeare's London

In Shakespeare's time Stratford-upon-Avon was a small country town with about 200 houses and fewer than a thousand inhabitants. London, about 100 miles away from Stratford, already had 200,000 inhabitants. Clearly it was a far more exciting place than Stratford. Theatres, for example, had become very fashionable in London. They were attended by people from all walks of life, from young apprentices to noblemen and kings. Between the opening of The Theatre in 1576 and that of the second Globe in 1614, London's citizens could choose from sixteen public and private theatres. Of these at least six were large public ones. Shakespeare's time was no doubt the greatest period of theatrical achievement in the history of Western civilization.

1. What London looked like

The south bank of the Thames. Detail of Hollar's View of London, 1647.

Map of London in Shakespeare's time.

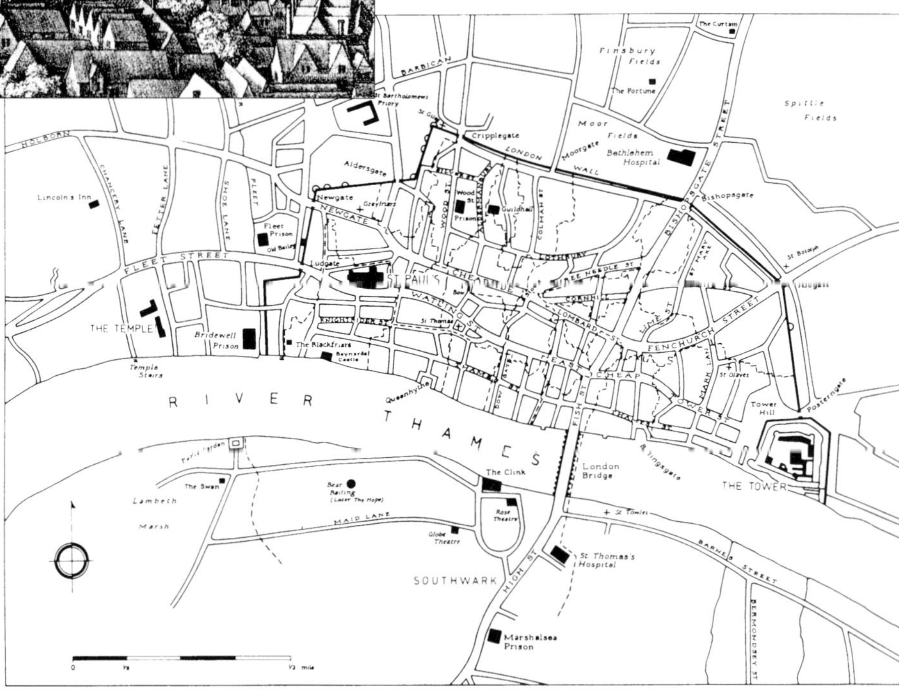

A closer look

1. What can you see in the drawing opposite? Give a detailed description.
2. a) List the buildings on the map that are, or might be, theatres.
   b) Look at the boundaries of central London (the dark line) and say where most of the theatres were situated.
3. Compare the map with the picture. Can you find any discrepancies?

2. A German traveller reports

A German traveller in Shakespeare's day kept a diary. He had this to say about entertainment in London:

Without the city are some theatres, where English actors represent almost every day comedies and tragedies to very numerous audiences; these are concluded with variety of dances, accompanied by excellent music and the excessive applause of those that are present.

There is still another place, built in the form of a theatre, which serves for the baiting of bears and bulls. They are fastened behind, and then worried by those great English dogs and mastiffs, but not without great risk to the dogs from the teeth of the one and the horns of the other; and it sometimes happens they are killed upon the spot. Fresh ones are immediately supplied in the places of those that are wounded or tired. To this entertainment there often follows that of whipping a blinded bear, which is performed by five or six men, standing in a circle with whips, which they exercise upon him without any mercy. Although he cannot escape from them because of his chain, he nevertheless defends himself, vigorously throwing down all who come within his reach and are not active enough to get out of it, and tearing the whips out of their hands and breaking them.

At these spectacles and everywhere else, the English are constantly smoking the Nicotian weed which in America is called *Tobaca* – others call it *Paetum* – and generally in this manner; they have pipes on purpose made of clay, into the farther end of which they put the herb, so dry that it may be rubbed into powder, and lighting it, they draw the smoke into their mouths, which they puff out again through their nostrils, like funnels, along with plenty of phlegm and defluxion from the head. In these theatres, fruits, such as apples, pears and nuts, according to the season, are carried about to be sold, as well as wine and ale.

From Paul Hentzner, Travels in England *(1598).*

1 **without** *here:* outside
8 **to bait** to make an animal angry intentionally
9 **to worry** *here:* to annoy
10 **mastiff** ['--] type of dog, large and strong
16 **to whip** to hit with a long piece of leather
19 **mercy** kindness
29 **on purpose** *here:* for that purpose
29 **clay** heavy, firm earth, also used for making pots etc.
30 **herb** plant that adds flavour, e.g. thyme
33 **nostrils** openings in the nose
33 **funnel** *here:* chimney
34 **phlegm** [flem] substance produced in the nose and throat when s.o. has a cold
34 **defluxion** *(old use)* spitting out of phlegm
37 **ale** *here:* beer in general

Bear-baiting

A closer look

1. What does Paul Hentzner say about:
   a) theatre performances
   b) theatre audiences c) bear baiting?
2. What do you think was so entertaining about bear-baiting?

3. A letter to the Archbishop

Not everybody was happy with the theatres. The Mayor of London wrote to the Archbishop to complain. What do you think the Mayor might have said to the Archbishop? How might he have tried to get help from the church leader?
The letter is not easy for us to read today. Note down the main points as you read.

Our most humble duties to Your Grace remembered. Whereas by the daily and disorderly exercise of a number of players and playing houses erected within this City, the youth thereof is greatly corrupted and their manners infected with many evil and ungodly qualities by reason of the wanton and profane devises represented on the stages by the said players, the apprentices and servants withdrawn from their works, and all sorts in general from the daily resort unto sermons and other Christian exercises to the great hindrance of the trades and traders of this City and profanation of the good and godly religion established amongst us. To which places also do usually resort great numbers of light and lewd-disposed persons as harlots, cutpurses, cozeners, pilferers, and such like and there under the colour of resort to those places to hear the plays devise divers evil and ungodly matches, confederacies and conspiracies, which by means of the opportunity of the place cannot be prevented nor discovered, as otherwise they might be. In consideration whereof we most humbly beseech Your Grace ... to vouchsafe us your good favor and help for the reforming and banishing of so great evil out of this City, which ourselves of long time though to small purpose have so earnestly desired and endeavored by all means that possibly we could.

Sir William Roe
Lord Mayor of the City of London
25 February 1592

1 **our ... remembered** *formal opening to letter, showing respect*
2 **whereas** common formula used in introductions to laws, petitions, etc.
3 **player** actor
7 **wanton** ['--] morally uncontrolled
7 **devise** = **device** *here:* story, action of a play
8 **apprentice** [ə'prentɪs] person learning a trade
9 **to withdraw** [-'-] to take away
10 **resort unto sermons** *(old use)* attendance at church
11 **hindrance** s.th. that stops s.th. or s.o. else from working well
15 **lewd-disposed** *(old use)* immoral, obscene
16 **harlot** ['--] *(old use)* prostitute
16 **cutpurse** *(old use)* pickpocket
16 **cozener** ['kʌznə] *(old use)* s.o. who cheats and deceives by trickery
16 **pilferer** *(old use)* thief
17 **under the colour of resort** *(old use) here:* pretending to visit
19 **match** *here:* forming of pairs
19 **confederacy** group of people joined for a certain purpose
19 **conspiracy** plan made by a group to do something unlawful
23 **to beseech** *(old use)* to ask urgently
23 **to vouchsafe** *(old use)* to promise
27 **to endeavor** *(usually* endeavour) [ɪn'devə] to try

A closer look
1. List the Mayor's complaints about the theatre in your own words.
2. Having seen where most London theatres were located, can you now think why this was so?
3. a) What similarities are there between these two descriptions of Elizabethan audiences (i.e. Paul Hentzner's and the Mayor's)?
   b) What two different purposes do they serve?
   c) Which text seems to give the more objective account?

In your opinion
What sort of performances and other recreational events might city-dwellers protest about today?

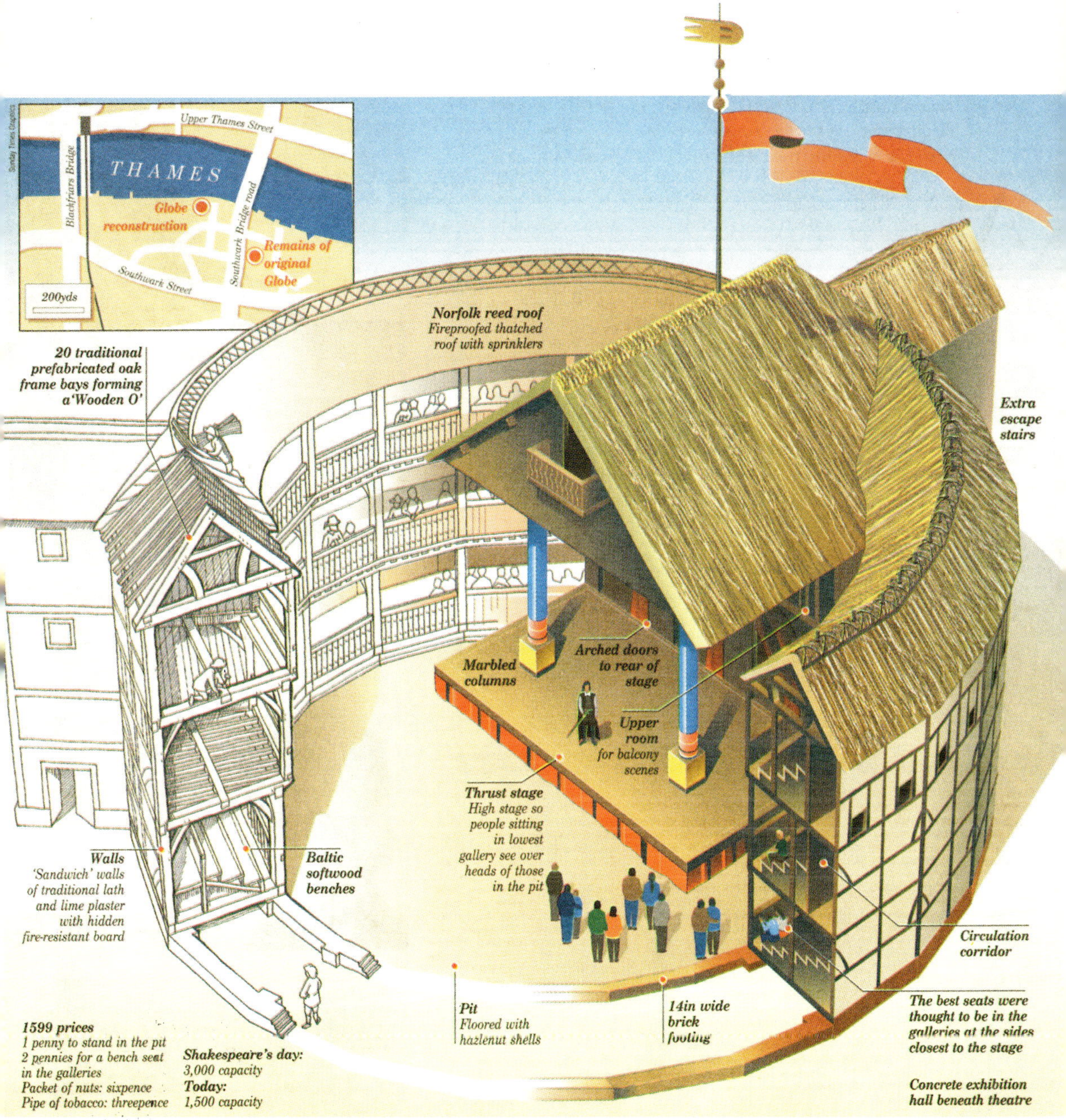

Cross-section of the new Globe Theatre as it has been constructed on the south bank of the Thames (see photo on page 15); from The Sunday Times, The Culture, *30th July, 1995.*

4. The Globe audience

The Globe audiences probably represented a wider range of citizens than have attended theatres in Britain since that time. The cost of admission was low, to attract as large a number as possible. The 'groundlings', who stood on the ground in the orchestra where there were no seats, were made up for the most parts of shopkeepers, craftsmen and

6 **orchestra** ['---] *here:* the main area of the theatre, at ground level

7 **craftsman** skilled workman, e. g. carpenter, goldsmith

members of what might be called the lower bourgeoisie.

There were also the apprentices, rowdy young men given to exhibitionism and liable to create disturbances out of sheer exuberance of spirit, but genuine lovers of the theatre, and usually well educated. There were also gentlemen of various degrees, professional men, courtiers, and members of the nobility. They would occupy twopenny or threepenny seats in the gallery. The higher members of the nobility would present themselves conspicuously in seats at the side of the stage itself or in shilling 'rooms'. Women were among the audience, often the respectable wives of tradesmen, a fact which surprised foreign visitors to London. The capacity of the Globe was probably about two thousand or a little more, and a typical audience would consist of at least one thousand people. Puritan enemies of the theatre insisted that people came there to make assignations and carry on immoral activities; but although a minority may have done this, there can be no doubt whatever that the large bulk of the audience came to enjoy the play.

From Literary Landscapes of the British Isles *by David Daiches and John Flower, New York and London: Paddington Press, 1979, p. 39.*

11 **exhibitionism** behaviour of a person who wants to be looked at and admired
12 **sheer** pure
12 **exuberance** [ɪg'zju:bərəns] state of being very lively and cheerful
15 **courtier** noble at the court of a king
16 **twopenny** ['tʌpnɪ]
17 **threepenny** ['θrepənɪ]
18 **conspicuously** attracting attention
20 **shilling** ten pence (old currency)
27 **assignation** *(formal)* secret meeting (e.g. with a lover)
30 **bulk** majority

Ball game, *1634, from* Emblems *by George Wither. This game may look harmless, but it was actually very rough and sometimes led to injury.*

A closer look
List all the groups of people that made up a typical audience at the Globe Theatre and say where each group sat or stood.

In your opinion
Clearly in Elizabethan times people from all classes of society went to the theatre. How does this compare with theatre audiences in your country today?

5. The background to popular taste

In Elizabethan times some plays were written for academics and the nobility, but most were written for commercial theatres such as The Globe, whose audiences were mixed and in which the 'groundlings' paid a penny for standing room.

... it was the groundlings who saved the drama from academic stiffness and preserved its essential bias towards entertainment – towards a high-spirited entertainment which was also criticism of life. [...]

The taste of the groundlings shows a striking elasticity. Without abandoning their old favourites,

2 **to preserve** to keep
2 **bias** ['baɪəs] tendency, leaning
3 **high-spirited** full of fun, lively
6 **to abandon** [ə'bændən] to give up

The Marriage Feast at Bermondsey *by Joris Hoefnagel (1542–1600). Bermondsey is now an inner suburb of London. Describe the activities you can make out in the painting.*

they were ready to welcome new themes of classical inspiration […]. They made Shakespeare, too, an immediate box-office success. […] Hamlet provides an outstanding instance of the groundlings' quickness of response. Its success was prompt and lasting, not only with 'the wiser sort' at the Universities (1601), but with 'all', and especially in 'the vulgar's Element' (1604). And this relation to the groundlings was vital to Shakespeare's work, both practically and artistically.

It was vital to the whole evolution of the drama. Literary playwrights borrowed freely from popular sources, from folk traditions as such, or from material already familiar through older plays, sermons, street ballads or pamphlets.

From "The Elizabethan Literary Renaissance" by L.G. Salingar, in: The Pelican Guide to English Literature, *edited by Boris Ford, Vol. 2:* The Age of Shakespeare, *Harmondsworth: Penguin Books, 1955, pp. 54–55.*

8 **classical** *here:* ancient Greek and Roman

8 **inspiration** source of ideas and themes

9 **box-office success** commercial success *(from* **box office** place at the theatre where tickets are sold)

14 **in 'the vulgar's Element'** among the common people

15 **vital** ['vaɪtl] extremely important

21 **sermon** speech made by a minister of religion on a religious theme

A closer look

1. What contribution did the groundlings make to Elizabethan drama?
2. What popular sources did the playwrights draw on?

4 A Survey of Shakespeare's Plays

Before you read the following, take a sheet of paper and note down all you know about individual plays of Shakespeare: titles, characters, plays that have been filmed, basic plots, a well-known line ... Then combine this information in class, perhaps on the board or on a sheet of paper on the wall.

William Shakespeare was in his twenties and a professional actor in London when he started writing plays for his theatre group. In the following twenty years he wrote 36 plays altogether – that is about two plays a year! He was obviously a very creative man, and there was clearly a demand for new plays. Here is a list of Shakespeare's plays. This is the probable order in which they were written, with some of the known dates. Not all scholars agree on the order or the dates.

1591 Henry VI (Parts 1, 2 and 3)
Richard III
Titus Andronicus
Love's Labours Lost
The Two Gentlemen of Verona
The Comedy of Errors
The Taming of the Shrew

1594 Romeo and Juliet
A Midsummer Night's Dream
Richard II
King John
The Merchant of Venice

1597 Henry IV (Parts 1 and 2)
Much Ado About Nothing
Merry Wives of Windsor
As You Like It
Julius Caesar
Henry V
Troilus and Cressida

1601 Hamlet
Twelfth Night
Measure for Measure
All's Well That Ends Well
Othello

1606 King Lear
Macbeth
Timon of Athens
Antony and Cleopatra
Coriolanus

1609 Pericles

1611 Cymbeline
The Winter's Tale
The Tempest
Henry VIII

A closer look

1. Draw up a table with the following headings:

Comedies	Classical themes (ancient Greek and Roman)	History (other than classical) and stories of Sh.'s day

2. Try to work out which category each play belongs to by just looking at the title. Enter them in the table using a pencil – that way you can correct any incorrect guesses later.
3. Examine the biographical table on page 6 in the light of the list of plays above.
   a) When did Shakespeare stop writing plays?
   b) What events coincided with the period of his greatest literary activity?

5 Some Well-Known Passages and Ideas

I didn't sleep a wink last night.
It's high time I left.
For goodness' sake!
I was tongue-tied at the interview.
She's a tower of strength to me.
I'm afraid that plant's as dead as a doornail.

The plays and poetry of William Shakespeare are the biggest source of quotations in the English language, if the "Oxford Dictionary of Quotations" is anything to go by. It cites 75 pages of his writing as quotations. That is almost twice as many as from the second biggest source, The Bible. Here is a selection of well-known passages from Shakespeare's work.

1. Thoughts about the theatre

William Shakespeare was not only a playwright but also an actor and – later – director and owner/shareholder of a theatre company in London. Even today, in the age of electronic media, the theatre has an impact on people. Actors on a stage can make a writer's ideas come alive. But is it only the actors? Who really makes things come alive on stage – the writer of the play, the actors, or the spectators' imagination? Shakespeare had very modern thoughts about such "invention" (i.e. the creation of an imaginary world), as the Prologue to Henry V *shows. Read the passage several times before you answer the questions.*

In Henry V, *Shakespeare refers to his theatre, The Globe, as the "wooden O". This picture shows the new Globe Theatre in July 1995 (see cross-section on page 11).*

CHORUS

O for a muse of fire, that would ascend
The brightest heaven of invention,
A kingdom for a stage, princes to act,
And monarchs to behold the swelling scene.
Then should the warlike Harry, like himself,
Assume the port of Mars, and at his heels,
(Leashed in, like hounds) should famine, sword, and fire
Crouch for employment. But pardon, gentles all,
The flat unraisèd spirits, that hath dared,
On this unworthy scaffold, to bring forth
So great an object. Can this cockpit hold
The vasty fields of France? Or may we cram
Within this wooden O the very casques
That did affright the air at Agincourt?
Oh, pardon: since a crooked figure may
Attest in little place a million,
And let us, ciphers to this great account,
On your imaginary forces work.
Suppose within the girdle of these walls
Are now confined two mighty monarchies,
Whose high uprearèd and abutting fronts
The perilous narrow ocean parts asunder.
Piece out our imperfections with your thoughts.
Into a thousand parts divide one man,
And make imaginary puissance.
Think when we talk of horses that you see them
Printing their proud hoofs i'th' receiving earth,
For 'tis your thoughts that now must deck our kings,
Carry them here and there, jumping o'er times,
Turning th'accomplishment of many years
Into an hour-glass. For the which supply
Admit me Chorus to this history,
Who, Prologue-like, your humble patience pray,
Gently to hear, kindly to judge our play.

1 **to ascend** [-'-] to move upwards
4 **to behold** *(old use)* to see, to look at
4 **swelling scene** *here:* development of the plot
5 **Harry** *here:* Henry V
6 **to assume** *here:* to take on, to use
6 **port** *here:* manner, style
6 **Mars** god of war
6 **at his heels** straight behind him
7 **to leash in** to tie down or control
8 **to crouch** to lower the body close to the ground, ready to jump
8 **for employment** ready for action
8 **gentles** *(old use)* ladies and gentlemen
9 **flat unraisèd spirits** *here:* actors *(the speaker suggests they are untalented)*
10 **scaffold** ['--] *here:* stage
11 **object** ['--] *here:* the play
11 **cockpit** small space *here:* stage
12 **vasty** [ɑ:] *(old use)* very large
12 **to cram** to make fit into a small space
13 **casque** [kæsk] *here:* helmet
14 **Agincourt** ['ædʒɪnkɔ:t] famous battle site (1415) in the Hundred Years' War
15 **crooked figure** ['krʊkɪd] badly written number
16 **to attest** *here:* to represent
17 **cipher** ['saɪfə] *here:* sign
18 **imaginary forces** powers of imagination
19 **girdle** belt, s.th. that encircles s.th.
20 **to confine** [-'-] to enclose
21 **uprearèd** on its back legs, ready to attack
21 **to abut** to border on
22 **perilous** dangerous
22 **asunder** apart
23 **to piece out** *here:* to correct
25 **puissance** ['pju:sns] *(old use)* power
28 **to deck** *(old use)* to decorate, to clothe
30 **accomplishment** [ə'kʌmplɪʃmənt] *here:* event
31 **hour-glass** glass container filled with sand, used for measuring time
31 **for the which supply** for this purpose
32 **admit me Chorus** let me be the Chorus (i.e. allow me to comment on events)
33 **to pray** *here:* to beg, to ask

A closer look

1. The first four lines of the prologue express a wish. What is it?
2. The speaker first voices the possible scepticism of the audience (ll. 11–14), then argues against it (ll. 15–18). Write down his argument in your own words.
3. What are the "imperfections" (l. 23) of the theatre? How is the audience expected to make up for them (ll. 23ff.)?

Scene from a film version of Henry V. *Considering what you have just read, do you think Shakespeare would have been happy to see* Henry V *turned into a film? Why, or why not?*

A look at the language

1. Look at the syntax of lines 17–18. Compare it with German syntax. What do you notice? What might this tell us about the development of the English language?
2. a) For each of the words below, write down the meaning as Shakespeare uses it and its meaning in modern English. Then try to describe the underlying common principle, e.g.:

	Meaning in Shakespeare's English	Meaning in modern English
"invention"	work of the imagination	new mechanical device

Common principle: something that has been thought up for the first time

b) Now do the same with these words: *swelling, employment, scaffold, cockpit, girdle.*

2. Order and disorder: Ulysses' speech

The Great Chain of Being was a commonly held concept in Shakespeare's time: all phenomena were seen as being interrelated in a well-balanced, hierarchical structure or "degree". From God as the centre of creation to the angels and spirits and down to the visible world of human beings, everything – animals, plants, rocks and minerals – was part of a well-graded universe, a finely tuned harmony that must not be disturbed. In the play Troilus and Cressida *(Act I Scene 3 ll. 85–124) Ulysses describes this concept in the following way:*

The heavens themselves, the planets, and this centre,
Observe degree, priority, and place, [...]
O, when degree is shak'd,
Which is the ladder of all high designs,
The enterprise is sick! How could communities,
Degrees in schools, and brotherhoods in cities,
Peaceful commerce from dividable shores,
The primogenity and due of birth,
Prerogative of age, crowns, sceptres, laurels,
But by degree, stand in authentic place?
Take but degree away, untune that string,
And hark what discord follows! Each thing melts
In mere oppugnancy: the bounded waters
Should lift their bosoms higher than the shores,
And make a sop of all this solid globe;
Strength should be lord of imbecility,
And the rude son should strike his father dead;
Force should be right; or rather, right and wrong –
Between whose endless jar justice resides –
Should lose their names, and so should justice too.
Then everything includes itself in power,
Power into will, will into appetite;
And appetite, an universal wolf,
So doubly seconded with will and power,
Must make perforce an universal prey,
And last eat up himself.

1 **this centre** the Earth (i.e. the centre of the universe)
2 **to observe** *here:* to follow, to obey
2 **place** *here:* position in the hierarchy
3 **shak'd** *(old use)* shaked, i.e. shaken
4 **ladder** *here:* hierarchical order of rank
5 **enterprise** plan, undertaking
6 **brotherhood** *here:* organization of people in the same profession (guild)
7 **dividable** *here:* separated
8 **primogenity** system by which all possessions pass from the father to the eldest son
8 **due of birth** *here:* right to privileges because of being the eldest son
9 **prerogative** [-'---] special right
9 **laurel** ['lɒrəl] *here:* honour won for achievements
10 **but** except; only
12 **to hark** *(old use)* to listen
12 **discord** ['--] disagreement, conflict
13 **mere** only
13 **oppugnancy** *(old use)* unfriendly, aggressive behaviour
13 **bounded** enclosed
14 **bosom** ['bʊzəm] breast; *here:* themselves
15 **sop** piece of bread soaked in milk, etc.; *here:* the earth swept by floods
16 **imbecility** complete stupidity
19 **jar** *here:* opening
19 **to reside** to live (in a place)
24 **to second** ['--] to assist, to support
25 **perforce** *(old use)* necessarily

A closer look

1. What parallels does Ulysses draw between the cosmic order and the social order?
2. What does he say will happen (in general) if the order within society is disturbed?
3. Can you think of any other works of literature – in English or in your own language – in which the natural order and the social order are linked in this way, i.e. in which natural (and social) catastrophes occur as a result of an imbalance in the order of society?

In your opinion

1. a) What kind of "classification" or "degree" can you recognize in your own society, and what criteria of belonging (birth, education, age ...) apply?
   b) Describe the similarities and differences between the criteria Shakespeare mentions for ordering society and those you feel apply in your society today.
2. Which aspects of Shakespeare's idea of "degree" could you accept from your modern point of view, and which not (say why not)?

3. England

Ever since the Norman invasion in 1066 Britain has not been conquered by external powers. Those 30-odd miles of water between Dover and Calais seem to have provided protection against all European aggressors. Thus the maintenance of British independence has been a leading feature of British politics through the centuries. Consider Britain's objections to many aspects of the European Community. What sort of arguments are used? Can you name a concrete example? Talk about this in class before you read on.
In Shakespeare's Richard II *(Act II Scene 1 ll. 40–68) the king's uncle, John of Gaunt, criticizes the frivolous extravagance of his nephew that has made it necessary to lease out the land (i.e. allow people to use it against payment) in order to raise money for the wars in Ireland:*

This royal throne of kings, this sceptered isle,
This earth of majesty, this seat of Mars,
This other Eden, demi-paradise,
This fortress built by Nature for herself
Against infection and the hand of war,
This happy breed of men, this little world,
This precious stone set in the silver sea
Which serves it in the office of a wall
Or as a moat defensive to a house
Against the envy of less happier lands,
This blessed plot, this earth, this realm, this England, [...]
This land of such dear souls, this dear, dear land,
Dear for her reputation through the world,
Is now leased out, I die pronouncing it,
Like to a tenement or pelting farm.
England, bound in with the triumphant sea
Whose rocky shore beats back the envious siege
Of watery Neptune, is now bound in with shame,
With inky blots and rotten parchment bonds,
That England that was wont to conquer others
Hath made a shameful conquest of itself.
Ah, would the scandal vanish with my life,
How happy then were my ensuing death!

1 **sceptered** ['septəd] *here:* royal
3 **demi-paradise** like paradise
4 **fortress** place that is difficult to attack
5 **infection** *here:* destructive influence
6 **breed** *here:* group with certain characteristics
7 **precious stone** stone of great worth (e.g. diamond)
8 **office** *here:* function
9 **moat** deep, wide channel of water around a building
11 **realm** [relm] land ruled by a monarch
15 **tenement** land that is rented, not owned
15 **pelting** *here:* insignificant
17 **siege** [si:dʒ] attempt to capture s.th. by surrounding it
19 **inky** of a substance that is used for writing with a pen
19 **blot** unwanted drop of liquid (e.g. ink) on paper
19 **rotten** completely spoiled
19 **parchment** old form of paper
19 **bond** binding agreement
20 **was wont to** used to
23 **ensuing** following

"...Whose rocky shore beats back the envious siege ..."
The white cliffs of Dover.

A closer look

1. In John of Gaunt's speech Shakespeare underlines a central aspect of English national identity, one that has hardly changed in the 400 years that have followed. What is it?
2. On several occasions in its history Britain has been in danger of being conquered by continental powers: in 1588, (when Shakespeare was a young man), between 1810 and 1812, and again in 1940. What were these powers, and who were their leaders?

A step further

1. Give one up-to-date example of Britain's unwillingness to hand over power – be it military, economic or political – to the European Community.

4. Three love sonnets

Shakespeare's Sonnets were first published in 1609 and comprise 154 poems. The exact circumstances of their creation remain one of the most fascinating mysteries of literary history. Apart from the play Hamlet *they are the topic most frequently discussed by Shakespeare scholars. Today it is generally agreed that Shakespeare wrote these sonnets between 1590 and 1594. The poems were written for a patron of Shakespeare, the young Henry Wriothesley, Earl of Southampton. Some of the poems seem to be highly autobiographical. The following selection of three sonnets all deal with various aspects of a very human experience:* ***love.***

Before you read the sonnets, do the following exercise:

1. Write down all the statements you can think of that you might hear in connection with the idea of love, e.g. "Love is blind". These might be partly your own thoughts, partly themes of literature and films you know, and common opinions. Include thoughts about how a person feels who is in love.
2. Hold a brainstorming in which you combine everyone's ideas, e.g. on a large sheet of paper. When you read the sonnets, see if you can find any of these ideas in them.

Sonnet 116

Let me not to the marriage of true minds
Admit impediments. Love is not love
Which alters when it alteration finds,
Or bends with the remover to remove.
O, no! it is an ever-fixed mark,
That looks on tempests and is never shaken;
It is the star to every wand'ring bark,
Whose worth's unknown, although his height be taken.
Love's not Time's fool, though rosy lips and cheeks
Within his bending sickle's compass come;
Love alters not with his brief hours and weeks,
But bears it out even to the edge of doom.
If this be error, and upon me prov'd,
I never writ, nor no man ever lov'd.

1 **marriage** *here:* unity
2 **to admit** *here:* to allow to enter
2 **impediment** s.th. which stops s.th. else from developing
3 **to alter** ['ɔ:ltə] to change
4 **to remove** *here:* to change
5 **mark** *here:* signal for ships
6 **tempest** *(old use)* storm
7 **bark** sailing ship with 3 masts
8 **taken** *here:* measured
10 **compass** ['kʌmpəs] *here:* reach, i.e. area of effectiveness
12 **to bear s.th. out** to be strong and patient despite difficulties
12 **doom** final disaster, end of the world (death)
13 **to prove** *here:* to demonstrate

Henry Wriothesley, 3rd Earl of Southampton (1573–1624), in a portrait attributed to John Decritz, the Elder (c. 1552–1642). The Earl was one of Shakespeare's strongest supporters and a very good friend.

A closer look

1. List the metaphors for love in the sonnet.
2. What does Shakespeare say love is *not*?

Sonnet 91

Some glory in their birth, some in their skill,
Some in their wealth, some in their body's force;
Some in their garments, though new-fangled ill;
Some in their hawks and hounds, some in their horse;
And every humour hath his adjunct pleasure,
Wherein it finds a joy above the rest;
But these particulars are not my measure:
All these I better in one general best.
Thy love is better than high birth to me,
Richer than wealth, prouder than garments' cost,
Of more delight than hawks or horses be;
And, having thee, of all men's pride I boast –
Wretched in this alone, that thou mayst take
All this away, and me most wretched make.

1 **to glory in** to be very proud of
1 **birth** *here:* social class s.o. is born into
3 **garments** clothes
3 **new-fangled** new but neither necessary nor better
3 **ill** *here:* unattractive, of poor quality
4 **hawk** bird which catches small animals; used in Shakespeare's day by hunters
4 **hound** hunting dog
5 **humour** *here:* type of personality
5 **adjunct** ['ædʒʌʌŋkt] added to s.th.
7 **measure** standard
8 **to better** to improve on
13 **wretched** ['retʃɪd] very unhappy, in very low spirits.

A closer look

1. Write down what Shakespeare is saying in each stanza in one short sentence.
2. How does the mood of the sonnet change in the rhyming couplet (two concluding lines, separate from the stanza before them, with end rhyme)?

In your opinion

1. What sort of things are people proud of today, as signs of status – i.e. what would you place in the first stanza from today's point of view?

Sonnet 27

Weary with toil, I haste me to my bed,
The dear repose for limbs with travel tired;
But then begins a journey in my head
To work my mind when body's work's expired;
For then my thoughts, from far where I abide,
Intend a zealous pilgrimage to thee,
And keep my drooping eyelids open wide,
Looking on darkness which the blind do see;
Save that my soul's imaginary sight
Presents thy shadow to my sightless view,
Which, like a jewel hung in ghastly night,
Makes black night beauteous and her old face new.
 Lo, thus, by day my limbs, by night my mind,
 For thee, and for myself, no quiet find.

1 **toil** *(old use)* hard work
2 **repose** *(old use)* rest
2 **limb** [lɪm] leg or arm
to expire to come to an end
4 **to abide** *(old use)* to stay or live (in
5 a place)
zealous ['zeləs] highly motivated
6 **pilgrimage** journey to a holy place
6 as an act of religious faith
thee *(old use)* you
6 **to droop** to hang down
7 **save** *here:* except
9 **ghastly** ['gɑːstlɪ] horrible, extremely
11 unpleasant
13 **lo** *(old use, exclamation)* see
13 **thus** in this way

A closer look
1. Who is the poet addressing?
2. Briefly summarize the message of this sonnet.

Review
1. Which of the sonnets do you like the most?
2. Write out one of the sonnets in modern English prose (not worrying about rhyme).
3. Learn one of the sonnets off by heart so that you are able to recite it.

In your opinion
1. Are Shakespeare's thoughts about love different from yours? Is his understanding of love antiquated or up-to-date? Discuss.

5. Man and woman

In the comedy The Taming of the Shrew *(Act V Scene 2 ll. 130–180) Shakespeare shows how Petruchio tries to tame his wife Katherina, who is known for her difficult temper. For a long time it is an open battle, a "war of the sexes", until in the end Katherina is tamed – or at least pretends to be. The test takes place at a family reunion at Katherina's parents' house. At her husband's command Katherina criticizes the other women for their disobedience.*

Elizabeth Taylor as Katherina and Richard Burton as Petruchio in a 1966 version of The Taming of the Shrew.

PETRUCHIO
Katherine, I charge thee, tell these headstrong women
What duty they do owe their lords and husbands.
WIDOW
Come, come, you're mocking. We will have no telling.
PETRUCHIO
Come on, I say, and first begin with her.
WIDOW
She shall not.
PETRUCHIO
I say she shall. And first begin with her.

shrew *here:* bad-tempered woman
1 **to charge** *here (old use):* to order
3 **to mock** to make a joke of s.o.

KATHERINA

Fie, fie, unknit that threatening, unkind brow,
And dart not scornful glances from those eyes
To wound thy lord, thy king, thy governor.
It blots thy beauty as frosts do bite the meads,
Confounds thy fame as whirlwinds shake fair buds,
And in no sense is meet or amiable.
A woman moved is like a fountain troubled,
Muddy, ill-seeming, thick, bereft of beauty,
And while it is so, none so dry or thirsty
Will deign to sip, or touch one drop of it.
Thy husband is thy lord, thy life, thy keeper,
Thy head, thy sovereign; one that cares for thee
And for thy maintenance; commits his body
To painful labour both by sea and land,
To watch the night in storms, the day in cold,
Whilst thou li'st warm at home, secure and safe,
And craves no other tribute at thy hands
But love, fair looks, and true obedience –
Too little payment for so great a debt.
Such duty as the subject owes the prince,
Even such a woman oweth to her husband.
And when she is froward, peevish, sullen, sour,
And not obedient to his honest will,
What is she but a foul contending rebel
And graceless traitor to her loving lord?
I am ashamed that women are so simple
To offer war where they should kneel for peace,
Or seek for rule, supremacy, and sway,
When they are bound to serve, love, and obey.
Why are our bodies soft, and weak, and smooth,
Unapt to toil and trouble in the world,
But that our soft conditions and our hearts
Should well agree with our external parts?
Come, come, you froward and unable worms,
My mind hath been as big as one of yours,
My heart as great, my reason haply more,
To bandy word for word and frown for frown.
But now I see our lances are but straws,
Our strength as weak, our weakness past compare,
That seeming to be most which we indeed least are.
Then vail your stomachs, for it is no boot,
And place your hands below your husband's foot.
In token of which duty, if he please,
My hand is ready, may it do him ease.

PETRUCHIO

Why, there's a wench! Come on, and kiss me, Kate.

7 **Fie** *(old use)* Shame!
7 **brow** *here (lit.):* forehead
8 **to dart** *here:* to throw s.th. sharp with sudden force
8 **scornful** showing disrespect
8 **glance** quick look
10 **to blot** to make an unattractive mark
10 **mead** [i:] *here:* large area of grass (meadow)
11 **to confound** to cause to be less easily seen
11 **whirlwind** strong wind moving in spirals
11 **bud** flower before opening
12 **meet** *(old use)* suitable, right
12 **amiable** ['eɪmjəbl] friendly
13 **moved** *here:* made angry
13 **fountain** ['--] *here:* deep hole full of water
13 **to trouble** *here:* to stir up
14 **bereft of** *(from* to bereave) without
16 **to deign** [deɪn] to lower oneself to do s.th.
19 **maintenance** ['meɪntənəns] financial support
23 **to crave** to desire s.th. greatly
28 **froward** ['frəʊəd] *(old use)* disobedient, rebellious
28 **peevish** dissatisfied, demanding
28 **sullen** ill-humoured, stubborn
30 **foul** *here:* with bad intentions
30 **to contend** [-'-] to struggle, to fight
31 **graceless** without respect
31 **traitor** s.o. who is not loyal
34 **to seek for** to look for
34 **sway** influence
35 **to be bound to** *here:* to have the obligation to
37 **unapt** *(old use)* unfit
37 **to toil** to work hard
42 **reason** *here:* ability to think logically
42 **haply** *(old use)* perhaps
43 **to bandy** to throw back and forth
44 **straw** piece of dry grass
45 **past compare** *(old use)* not worth comparing
47 **to vail one's stomach** *(old use)* to control one's passion and anger (the stomach was seen as the seat of the emotions)
47 **no boot** *here (old use):* no use
51 **wench** *(old use)* country girl or woman

A closer look

1. Why, according to Katherina in this speech, should women obey their husbands?
2. What is expected of husbands?
3. Why are women not meant to "toil and trouble in the world" (l. 31)?

In your opinion

1. How do you feel about the division of roles beween men and women that Katherina supports in this speech?
2. Scholars still debate as to whether Katherina really means what she is saying. If you were producing the play, what stage directions (placement of characters, gestures etc.) would you give the actors
   a) if you thought Katherina meant what she said in this scene
   b) if you thought she was just trying to please her husband.

Katherina and Petruchio present a harmonious picture to the world.

6. Government and society

You are already familiar with the idea of "order" and "degree" (see Ulysses' speech on pp. 17–18). In Henry V *(Act I Scene 2 ll. 178–213) Shakespeare outlines what this means in terms of the division of labour within society. The Archbishop of Canterbury is talking to Henry and his nobleman about the functioning of a state. As long as there is general consent, they argue, activities in society may vary greatly. Different people have different functions in society – yet, in the end, they all serve one purpose.*

EXETER

While that the armèd hand doth fight abroad
Th'advisèd head defends itself at home.
For government, though high and low and lower,
Put into parts, doth keep in one consent,
Congreeing in a full and natural close
Like music.

4 **consent** agreement
5 **to congree** to agree
5 **close** [kləʊz] end, conclusion

CANTERBURY

Therefore doth heaven divide
The state of man in diverse functions,
Setting endeavour in continual motion,
To which is fixèd as an aim or butt
Obedience. For so work the honey-bees
Creatures that by a rule in nature teach
The act of order to a peopled kingdom.
They have a king, and officers of sorts,
Where some like magistrates correct at home,
Others like merchants venture trade abroad,
Others like soldiers, armèd in their stings,
Make boot upon the summer's velvet buds,
Which pillage they with merry march bring home
To the tent royal of their emperor,
Who, busied in his majesties, surveys
The singing masons building roofs of gold,
The civil citizens kneading up the honey,
The poor mechanic porters crowding in
Their heavy burdens at his narrow gate,
The sad-eyed justice with his surly hum
Delivering o'er to executors pale
The lazy yawning drone. I this infer,
That many things, having full reference
To one consent, may work contrariously.
As many arrows, loosèd several ways
Fly to one mark; as many ways meet in one town,
As many fresh streams meet in one salt sea,
As many lines close in the dial's centre,
So may a thousand actions, once afoot
End in one purpose, and be all well borne
Without defeat.

9 **endeavour** [ɪn'devə] *here:* work, effort
9 **motion** movement
10 **butt** point that is aimed at
16 **to venture** to try to do successfully
17 **sting** ability to attack
18 **boot** (*usu.* booty) goods taken from the enemy after their defeat
18 **velvet** *here:* soft and smooth
18 **bud** leaf, flower or branch at the very beginning, before opening
19 **pillage** *see* boot
21 **to survey** [sə'veɪ] to view, to watch
22 **mason** person who works with stone
24 **mechanic** relating to manual work (work with the hands)
26 **justice** *here:* judge
26 **surly** ['sɜ:lɪ] bad-tempered, unfriendly
26 **hum** noise s.o. makes in his/her throat while thinking about s.th.
27 **executor** [-'---] s.o. who puts things into effect *(legal term)*
28 **to yawn** to open the mouth widely when one is tired or bored
28 **drone** *here:* monotonous voice
28 **to infer** [-'-] to conclude
29 **to have full reference** *here:* to concentrate fully on
30 **consent** *here:* aim
30 **contrariously** *here:* against each other
34 **dial** ['daɪəl] face of an instrument such as a clock or watch.

A closer look

1. What is the ideal state compared to?
2. The passage begins and ends with an important statement about the basis of every government. What is it?
3. a) Describe what you can see in the portrait of Queen Elizabeth I on the next page. What image of the Queen does it present?
   b) What do you think is the purpose of having a portrait painted in this manner?
   c) Which lines of Canterbury's speech reflect the image of royalty presented in this portrait?

In your opinion

1. Diversity of talents, unity of purpose. To what extent does this principle apply to the society you live in? Discuss.
2. a) How would you define the main role of government in a democratic state?
   b) Discuss the similarities and differences between your concept of the state and government and the one put forward in this text.

Queen Elizabeth I, in the so-called Armada portrait, version 2, attributed to George Gower (1540–1596).

6 Macbeth in the Limelight

In the course of history, opinions of, and reactions to, Shakespeare's art have changed considerably. In his own time he was considered a writer of popular plays but not a genius. Later, classical French writers such as Voltaire criticized Shakespeare for not observing the classic criteria of good playwriting, i.e. the unity of action, time and place. However, classical German writers such as Schiller, Goethe and others "rediscovered" Shakespeare, and the translation of Schlegel/Tieck almost made him into a German writer.
This section contains five extracts from contemporary writing which may help you to understand The Tragedy of Macbeth *better. The first one is a scene from a play, in which the protagonist sees* Macbeth *for the first time. The second text explains the concept of "the great chain of being", which is vital to an understanding of* Macbeth. *The other three texts are extracts from modern Shakespeare scholarship and criticism. They all have slightly different approaches to understanding the play.*

1. "It's fun, tragedy, isn't it?"

Willy Russell's play Educating Rita *tells the story of Rita, a hairdresser in her twenties living in the English Midlands. Rita decides to improve her education. She enrols in an Open University course, for which lectures are broadcast on television. Students also receive study materials to work through. Once a week she goes to her tutor Frank, a university lecturer.*
In Act I Scene 6 Rita pays Frank an unscheduled visit. Last night she saw a professional theatre performance for the first time in her life. It was Shakespeare's Macbeth. *Rita is so impressed that she has to tell Frank all about it.*

(Rita bursts through the door out of breath)

FRANK What are you doing here? *(He looks at his watch)* It's Thursday, you …

RITA *(moving over to the desk; quickly)* I know I shouldn't be here, it's me dinner hour, but listen, I've gorra tell someone, have y' got a few minutes, can y' spare …?

gorra *(dialect, slang)* got to
to spare to have (s.th.) left over

FRANK *(alarmed)* My God, what is it?

RITA I had to come an' tell y', Frank, last night, I went to the theatre! A proper one, a professional theatre.

Frank gets up and switches off the radio and then returns to the swivel chair.

swivel chair chair that can move in circles

FRANK *(sighing)* For God's sake, you had me worried, I thought it was something serious.

RITA No, listen, it was. I went out an' got me ticket, it was Shakespeare, I thought it was gonna be dead borin'…

gonna *(slang)* going to
dead *here (slang):* terribly

FRANK Then why did you go in the first place?

RITA I wanted to find out. But listen, it wasn't borin', it was bleedin' great, honest, ogh, it done me in, it was fantastic. I'm gonna do an essay on it.

bleedin' *(slang)* really
to do s.o. in *here (slang):* to impress s.o. deeply

FRANK *(smiling)* Come on, which one was it?

Rita moves URC

URC up right centre

RITA "… Out, out, brief candle !
Life's but a walking shadow, a poor player
That struts and frets his hour upon the stage
And then is heard no more. It is a tale
Told by an idiot, full of sound and fury
Signifying nothing."

to strut to walk stiffly and proudly
to fret to be very anxious

FRANK *(deliberately)* Ah, *Romeo and Juliet.*

deliberately with intention

RITA *(moving towards Frank)* Tch. Frank! Be serious. I learnt that today from the book. *(She produces a copy of "Macbeth")* Look, I went out an' bought the book. Isn't it great? What I couldn't get over is how excitin' it was.

Frank puts his feet up on the desk

Wasn't his wife a cow, eh? An' that fantastic bit where he meets Macduff an' he thinks he's all invincible. I was

invincible too strong to be defeated

"... that fantastic bit where he meets Macduff an' he thinks he's all invincible ..." Macbeth, *Act V Scene 8 (in a performance by the Royal Shakespeare Company, Stratford-upon-Avon, 1982).*

on the edge of me seat at that bit. I wanted to shout out an' tell Macbeth, warn him.

FRANK You didn't, did you?

RITA Nah. Y' can't do that in a theatre, can y'? It was dead good. It was like a thriller.

FRANK Yes. You'll have to go and see more.

RITA I'm goin' to. *Macbeth's* a tragedy, isn't it?

Frank nods.

Right.

Rita smiles at Frank and he smiles back at her
Well I just - I just had to tell someone who'd understand.

FRANK I'm honoured that you chose me.

RITA *(moving towards the door)* Well, I better get back. I've left a customer with a perm lotion. If I don't get a move on there'll be another tragedy.

FRANK No. There won't be a tragedy.

RITA There will, y' know. I know this woman; she's dead fussy. If her perm doesn't come out right there'll be blood an' guts everywhere.

fussy very concerned about details
perm permanent wave
blood an' guts signs of violence

FRANK Which might be quite tragic -
He throws her the apple from his desk which she catches
- but it won't be a tragedy.

RITA What?

FRANK Well - erm - look; the tragedy of the drama has nothing to do with the sort of tragic event you're talking about. Macbeth is flawed by his ambition - yes?

to be flawed to have a weakness
ambition strong desire for success, power, wealth etc.

RITA *(going and sitting in the chair by the desk)* Yeh. Go on. *(She starts to eat the apple)*

Julie Walters as Rita and Michael Caine as Frank, in the 1983 film version of Educating Rita.

FRANK Erm - it's that flaw which forces him to take the inevitable steps towards his own doom. You see?

inevitable [-'----] unable to be avoided
doom terrible fate, unavoidable destruction or death

Rita offers him the can of soft drink. He takes it and looks at it.

(Putting the can down on the desk) No thanks. Whereas, Rita, a woman's hair being reduced to an inch of stubble, or - or the sort of thing you read in the paper that's reported as being tragic, "Man Killed By Falling Tree", is not a tragedy.

stubble short, stiff pieces of s.th. (*here:* hair)

RITA It is for the poor sod under the tree.

sod *(slang)* person

FRANK Yes, it's tragic, absolutely tragic. But it's not a tragedy in the way that *Macbeth* is a tragedy. Tragedy in dramatic terms is inevitable, pre-ordained. Look, now, even without ever having heard the story of *Macbeth* you wanted to shout out, to warn him and prevent him going on, didn't you? But you wouldn't have been able to stop him would you?

pre-ordained planned (by God or fate) from the beginning
to prevent to stop

RITA No.

FRANK Why?

RITA They would have thrown me out the theatre.

FRANK But what I mean is that your warning would have been ignored. He's warned in the play. But he can't go back. He still treads the path to doom. But the poor old fellow under the tree hasn't arrived there by following any inevitable steps has he?

to tread to walk on

RITA No.

FRANK There's no particular flaw in his character that has dictated his end. If he'd been warned of the consequences of standing beneath that particular tree he wouldn't have done it, would he? Understand.

Rita So - so Macbeth brings it on himself?

FRANK Yes. You see he goes blindly on and on and with every step he's spinning one more piece of thread which will eventually make up the network of his own tragedy. Do you see?

thread [θred] very fine length of cotton (wool etc.) used for sewing or weaving

RITA I think so. I'm not used to thinkin' like this.

FRANK It's quite easy, Rita.

RITA It is for you. I just thought it was a dead excitin' story. But the way you tell it you make me see all sorts of things in it. *(After a pause)* It's fun, tragedy, isn't it?

From Educating Rita. A Comedy *by Willy Russell, London: Samuel French Ltd, 1981, pp. 27–29*

Macbeth "brings it on himself" – a scene from a Japanese film of Macbeth *entitled* The Throne of Blood *(produced by Kurosawa).*

A closer look

1. Characterize:
   a) Rita
   b) Frank.
2. What is the difference between 'tragic' and 'tragedy', according to Frank? (Frank's definition of 'tragedy' is a classic one, so you should remember it.)

A step further

1. a) Note all the details about *Macbeth* that we learn in this extract.
   b) Make up a storyline based on these details. Use your imagination!
2. If possible, watch a video or film of *Macbeth* (e.g. a BBC production – if your school does not have one, you could possibly borrow one from the British Council) or go to a theatre performance. Write down your reactions to this experience. Are they anything like Rita's?

2. The Macbeth Murder Mystery

"It was a stupid mistake to make," said the American woman I had met at my hotel in the English lake country, "but it was on the counter with the other Penguin books - the little six-penny ones, you know, with the paper covers - and I supposed of course it was a detective story. All the others were detective stories. I'd read all the others, so I bought this one without really looking at it carefully. You can imagine how mad I was when I found it was Shakespeare." I murmured something sympathetically. "I don't see why the Penguin-books people had to get out Shakespeare plays in the same size and everything as the detective stories," went on my companion. "I think they have different-colored jackets," I said. "Well, I didn't notice that," she said. "Anyway, I got really comfy in bed that night and all ready to read a good mystery story and here I had *The Tragedy of Macbeth* - a book for high-school students. Like *Ivanhoe*." ... "Or *Lorna Doone*," I said. "Exactly," said the American lady. "And I was just crazy for a good Agatha Christie, or something. Hercule Poirot is my favourite detective." "Is he the rabbity one ?" I asked. "Oh, no," said my crime-fiction expert. "He's the Belgian one. You're thinking of Mr. Pinkerton, the one that helps Inspector Bull. He's good, too."

Over her second cup of tea my companion began to tell the plot of a detective story that had fooled her completely - it seems it was the old family doctor all the time. But I cut in on her. "Tell me," I said. "Did you read *Macbeth* ?" "I *had* to read it," she said. "There wasn't a scrap of anything else to read in the whole room." "Did you like it ?" I asked. "No, I did not," she said, decisively. "In the first place, I don't think for a moment that Macbeth did it." I looked at her blankly.

English lake country Lake District in northern England

to murmur ['mɜːmə] to say s.th. very quietly and unclearly

comfy *(informal)* comfortable

Ivanhoe novel by Sir Walter Scott (1819)

Lorna Doone novel by R. D. Blackmore (1869)

scrap small piece

blankly without expression

Thurber himself did this drawing for the cover of his collection, A Thurber Carnival, *which contains our story.*

"Did what ?" I asked. "I don't think for a moment that he killed the King," she said. "I don't think the Macbeth woman was mixed up in it, either. You suspect them the most, of course, but those are the ones that are never guilty - or shouldn't be, anyway." "I'm afraid," I began, "that I -" "But don't you see ?" said the American lady. "It would spoil everything if you could figure out right away who did it. Shakespeare was too smart for that. I've read that people never *have* figured out *Hamlet*, so it isn't likely Shakespeare would have made *Macbeth* as simple as it seems." I thought this over while I filled my pipe. "Who do you suspect?" I asked, suddenly. "Macduff," she said, promptly. "Good God!" I whispered, softly.

"Oh, Macduff did it, all right," said the murder specialist. "Hercule Poirot would have got him easily." "How did you figure it out?" I demanded. "Well," she said, "I didn't right away. At first I suspected Banquo. And then, of course, he was the second person killed. That was good right in there, that part. The person you suspect of the first murder should always be the second victim." "Is that so ?" I murmured. "Oh, yes," said my informant. "They have to keep surprising you. Well, after the second murder I didn't know *who* the killer was for a while." "How about Malcolm and Donalbain, the King's sons?" I asked. "As I remember it, they fled right after the first murder. That looks suspicious." "Too suspicious," said the American lady. "Much too suspicious. When they flee, they're never guilty. You can count on that." "I believe," I said, "I'll have a brandy," and I summoned the waiter. My companion leaned toward me, her eyes bright, her teacup quivering. "Do you know who discovered Duncan's body?" she demanded. I said I was sorry, but I had forgotten. "Macduff discovers it," she said, slipping into the historical present. "Then he comes running downstairs and shouts, 'Confusion has broke open the Lord's anointed temple' and 'Sacrilegious murder has made his masterpiece' and on and on like that." The good lady tapped me on the knee. "All that stuff was rehearsed," she said. "You wouldn't say a lot of stuff like that, offhand, would you - if you had found a body?" She fixed me with a glittering eye. "I –" I began. "You're right!" she said. "You wouldn't! Unless you had practiced it in advance. 'My God, there's a body in here!' is what an innocent man would say." She sat back with a confident glare.

I thought for a while. "But what do you make of the Third Murderer ?" I asked. "You know, the Third Murderer has puzzled *Macbeth* scholars for three hundred years." "That's because they never thought of Macduff," said the American lady. "It was Macduff, I'm certain. You couldn't have one of the victims murdered by two ordinary thugs - the murderer always has to be somebody important. " "But what about the banquet scene ?" I asked, after a moment. "How do you account for Macbeth's guilty actions there, when Banquo's ghost came in and sat in his chair ?" The lady leaned forward and tapped me on the knee again. "There

to summon to call, to send for
to quiver to shake
to anoint to select ceremonially for a holy task or calling
sacrilegious [ˌsækrɪˈlɪdʒəs] violating or showing disrespect for s.th. holy
to rehearse to practise (a play etc.) before the first performance
offhand as if not caring
to glitter to shine in many small points of light
confident sure of oneself
glare *here:* penetrating stare
thug violent criminal
to account for to explain

wasn't any ghost," she said. "A big, strong man like that doesn't go around seeing ghosts - especially in a brightly lighted banquet hall with dozens of people around. Macbeth was *shielding somebody*!" "Who was he shielding ?" I asked. "Mrs. Macbeth, of course," she said. "He thought she did it and he was going to take the rap himself. The husband always does that when the wife is suspected." "But what," I demanded, "about the sleepwalking scene, then ?" "The same thing, only the other way round," said my companion. "That time *she* was shielding *him*. She wasn't asleep at all. Do you remember where it says, 'Enter Lady Macbeth with a taper'?" "Yes," I said. "Well, people who walk in their sleep *never carry lights!*" said my fellow-traveler. "They have a second sight. Did you ever hear of a sleepwalker carrying a light ?" "No," I said, "I never did." "Well, then, she wasn't asleep. She was acting guilty to shield Macbeth." "I think," I said, "I'll have another brandy," and I called the waiter. When he brought it, I drank it rapidly and rose to go.

"I believe," I said, "that you have got hold of something. Would you lend me that *Macbeth* ? I'd like to look it over tonight. I don't feel, somehow, as if I'd ever really read it." "I'll get it for you," she said. "But you'll find that I'm right."

I read the play over carefully that night, and the next morning, after breakfast, I sought out the American woman. She was on the putting green, and I came up behind her silently and took her arm. She gave an exclamation. "Could I see you alone ?" I asked, in a low voice. She nodded cautiously and followed me to a secluded spot. "You've found out something?" she breathed. "I've found out," I said, triumphantly, "the name of the murderer!"

"You mean it wasn't Macduff ?" she said. "Macduff is as innocent of those murders," I said, "as Macbeth and the Macbeth woman." I opened the copy of the play, which I had with me, and turned to Act II, Scene 2. "Here," I said, "you will see where Lady Macbeth says, 'I laid their daggers ready. He could not miss'em. Had he not resembled my father as he slept, I had done it.' Do you see ?" "No," said the American woman, bluntly, "I don't." "But it's simple!" I exclaimed. "I wonder I didn't see it years ago. The reason Duncan resembled Lady Macbeth's father as he slept is that *it actually was her father!*" "Good God!" breathed my companion, softly. "Lady Macbeth's father killed the King," I said, "and, hearing someone coming, thrust the body under the bed and crawled into the bed himself." "But," said the lady, "you can't have a murderer who only appears in the story once. You can't have that." "I know that," I said, and I turned to Act II, Scene 4. "It says here 'Enter Ross with an old Man.' Now, that old man is never identified and it is my contention he was old Mr. Macbeth, whose ambition it was to make his daughter Queen. There you have your motive." "But even then," cried the American lady, "he's still a minor character!" "Not," I said, gleefully, "when you realize that he was also *one of the weird sisters in disguise!*" "You mean one of the three witches?"

to shield to protect
rap *(informal)* punishment
taper *here:* wax candle
putting green [ʌ] (*from* to putt) lawn on which golf is played
cautiously carefully
secluded isolated, hidden
to resemble to look like
bluntly abruptly, directly
contention point that one argues for
gleefully very happily
weird very strange
in disguise dressed to hide one's identity

The Three Witches in a production by the Royal Shakespeare Company in 1976.

"Precisely," I said. "Listen to this speech of the old man's. 'On Tuesday last, a falcon towering in her pride of place, was by a mousing owl hawk'd at and kill'd.' Who does that sound like?" "It sounds like the way the three witches talk," said my companion, reluctantly. "Precisely!" I said again. "Well," said the American woman, "maybe you're right, but –" "I'm sure I am," I said. "And do you know what I'm going to do now ?" "No," she said. "What ?" "Buy a copy of *Hamlet,*" I said, "and solve *that!*" My companion's eyes brightened. "Then," she said, "you don't think Hamlet did it?" "I am," I said, "absolutely positive he didn't." "But who," she demanded, "do you suspect?" I looked at her cryptically. "Everybody," I said, and disappeared into a small grove of trees as silently as I had come.

From My World – And Welcome To It *by James Thurber, New York: Harcourt, Brace & World, 1942.*

falcon bird that hunts small animals
to be hawked at to be hunted by a bird that hunts small animals
reluctantly unwillingly
cryptically with an air of mystery

A closer look

1. The American lady is an 'expert' on detective fiction. Collect all the statements she makes about a well-constructed detective story and say how she applies these rules to *Macbeth.*
2. What is the humour in this story based on? Give examples.
3. Apart from ridiculing one approach to Shakespeare, Thurber is making a point about the way in which we approach literature generally. What do you think it is?

A step further

Now you know more about *Macbeth.* Compare this to your own story (see p. 31).

3. The great chain of being

In Macbeth, Julius Caesar, Hamlet *and other plays by Shakespeare, we find that after upheaval, revolt and murder the play ends with the restoration of order. This order-disorder antithesis, which was the central theme of Ulysses' speech (**pp. 17–18**), is the subject of the picture below and the text following it.*

The Four Grades of Man, from C. Bovillus Liber de Sapiente *(1509).*

According to the conception of 'the great chain of being' we have, under God, in descending sequence, the categories of angelic beings, men, animals, plants, minerals. Angels are superior to men, men are superior to animals, animals to plants, plants to minerals. Minerals have being only: plants have something that minerals do not have - a vegetable soul - they grow: animals have being, and the power of growth, and also something else - a sensitive soul - they can see and feel, smell and taste and hear: men can do all that plants and animals can do, they grow, they sense, but in addition they have reason, which the animals do not have - man's reason marks him off clearly from the animals: angels, above men, are pure intelligence.

antithesis [-'---]
to descend to move downwards
vegetable *here:* belonging to plant life
sensitive *here:* having the five senses

This is a scale of categories. In each of these categories there are gradations also – among the minerals, for example, gold is higher in the scale than silver; among the plants the oak is higher in the scale than the elm; among men a king is higher than his subjects; among the angelic beings archangels are higher than ordinary angels; and so on. The whole of reality is a great hierarchy, a system of degrees, gradations: everything has its duly appointed place in it. Man, it will be observed, occupies a position between the angels and the beasts. His reason allies him to the angels: but, if he lets his reason go, then he becomes like a beast. ...

It is the duty of every created thing to maintain itself in its own duly appointed place in the hierarchy: it is a sin to aspire to occupy by force a higher position in the scale than one is entitled to, and it is equally a sin to occupy a lower position in the scale than one is entitled to. There is room in the scheme for evolution upwards: but forcible usurpation of a place in the scale other than one's own is a sin against the law of order, or 'degree' as Shakespeare calls it in *Troilus and Cressida*. We may speak of the law of order, or the law of degree: we may equally well speak of the law of nature, for, according to this conception of reality, order is natural, disorder unnatural. A subject who rebels against the king is producing disorder: he is also acting unnaturally.

From Shakespeare *by Ian Duthie, London: Hutchinson, 1951, pp. 41–42.*

subject *here:* person under someone's authority
archangel ['ɑːkˌeɪndʒəl]
duly appointed fixed according to a set pattern
to ally ['ælaɪ]
to maintain [-'-] to keep
to aspire to try to reach
to be entitled to to have a right to
usurpation [juːzɜː'peɪʃn] occupation of a position that is not yours

A closer look

1. Look at the illustration on the opposite page. Analyse the details as well as the overall composition. What is the relationship between the left and the right halves? Why are they made to correspond?
2. Sum up the characteristics of the 'great chain of being' described by Duthie.
3. a) How, according to Duthie, are human beings capable of disturbing this 'natural order'?
   b) Duthie refers to Ulysses' speech in *Troilus and Cressida* (pp. 17–18 . What happens, according to Ulysses – and Elizabethan thinking – when the natural order is turned upside down?
4. "There is only one theme in 'Macbeth': Murder. History has been reduced to its simplest form, to one image and one division – those who kill and those who are killed" (Jan Kott). According to Shakespeare scholar Kott, history becomes a nightmare in *Macbeth.* How does this relate to the order-disorder antithesis?

A step further

1. To many modern thinkers, such a hierarchical system seems very conservative. Look up the word 'conservative' and say whether you think it fits the Elizabethan world view. Give reasons for your opinion.
2. a) How is order created and maintained in the society you live in?
   b) What are seen to be the main causes of imbalances in society?
   c) How does the Elizabethan view of the causes of disorder differ from your own view and that of other individuals or groups in your society? Can you see any similarities?

4. The circular movement of the play

Macbeth centres around a single action - the murder of Duncan - which, like the action of Coriolanus and Antony, is seen as self-defeating. The whole structure of the play makes this clear: Scotland moves from health to sickness and back into health, Malcolm replaces Duncan, and the wheel comes full circle without Macbeth having made any permanent achievement. The energy he expends in trying to secure his position contrasts ironically with this lack of attainment: his actions are cancelled out by the circular movement of the play, and he becomes a momentary aberration in Scotland's history, an aberration without lasting consequence: the history rights itself and continues. Macbeth's action in killing Duncan is marred by a literal sterility: he will have no sons to make his achievement permanently fruitful. But the action is inherently sterile, too, and it is this paradox which the play builds on: an action intended as creative, self-definitive, is in fact destructive, self-undoing.

From Shakespeare and Society. Critical Studies in Shakespearean Drama *by Terence Eagleton, London: Chatto & Windus, 1970, p. 130.*

2 **Coriolanus and Antony** play by Shakespeare. Coriolanus' chances of success and happiness are ruined by his pride.
3 **self-defeating** preventing its own success
8 **to expend** to use up
9 **lack** absence
9 **attainment** achievement
10 **to cancel out** to negate
12 **aberration** sudden change away from the usual path
14 **to mar** to spoil
15 **literal** in a concrete way
17 **inherently** by its own nature
18 **self-definitive** defining itself
19 **self-undoing** self-destructive

A closer look

1. Explain in your own words what is meant by
   a) the 'circular movement' of the play
   b) the 'sterility' of Macbeth's actions.
2. Relate this description of the plot of *Macbeth* to the order-disorder antithesis (pp. 17–18).

In your opinion

1. Do you think the interpretation of history presented in Macbeth could in fact be realistic in certain situations? Give reasons for your answer, citing examples from world history.

*When Macbeth tries to seize power, the heavens are "troubled with man's act", as Ross remarks to an old man (*Macbeth, *Act II Scene 4). A director would have to try to put across the 'unnatural' atmosphere of this scene, which takes place at night. Here you see only the figures of Ross (right) and the old man – but still the picture gives you some clues as to how this director has achieved such an atmosphere. What are they?*

The Three Witches, in a film production, originally for television, by George Schaefer (Great Britain, 1960). Compare this interpretation of the witches to that on p. 35.

5. A study of evil

In *Macbeth* Shakespeare explored more fully and deeply than in any of his other plays the nature and effects of evil. It is portrayed in the action, particularly in the murder of Duncan and of Macduff's family, in the characters, most obviously that of Lady Macbeth, and in the dark, oppressive images which convey the impression of evil as a palpable, substantial presence:

Light thickens, and the crow
Makes wing to th'rooky wood;
Good things of day begin to droop and drowse,
Whiles night's black agents to their preys do rouse.

Now o'er the one half-world
Nature seems dead, and wicked dreams abuse
The curtain'd sleep; now witchcraft celebrates
Pale Hecate's offerings; and wither'd murder,
Alarum'd by his sentinel, the wolf,
Whose howl's his watch, thus with stealthy pace,
Moves like a ghost.

The potential for evil is present in the whole of creation: in nature, the animals and in man, all three of which are linked together in this second passage. It is also a supernatural force and, as such, is invoked by the witches in their spells and by Lady Macbeth when she calls upon the 'spirits that tend on mortal thoughts' to possess her totally.

6 **oppressive** negative, threatening
7 **palpable** ['pælpəbl] able to be touched physically; not abstract
9 **rooky** [ʊ] *(old use)* full of large, black birds (rooks)
9 **wood** *here:* forest
10 **to droop** [u:] to hang down due to age or tiredness (e.g. flowers)
10 **to drowse** to become sleepy
11 **prey** [eɪ] the creatures that an animal hunts in order to live
11 **to rouse** [raʊz] to become active
13 **to abuse** [ə'bu:z] to treat badly
14 **curtain'd** sheltered (beds often had curtains around them)
14 **witchcraft** skill of using magic powers, especially evil ones
15 **Hecate** ['--] goddess of witchcraft
15 **to wither** to dry out and die
16 **sentinel** ['---] s.o. who keeps watch
17 **stealthy** quiet, not wanting to be noticed
17 **pace** speed
22 **to invoke** *here:* to call on
23 **spell** *here:* magic formula producing supernatural effects
24 **to tend on** *(old use)* to work on
24 **mortal** of human beings

In The Tragedy of Doctor Faustus, *a play by Shakespeare's contemporary Christopher Marlowe (1564–1593), it is Mephistopholis who embodies the forces of evil. Like the witches in* Macbeth, *Mephistopholis persuades the protagonist to act according to his ambition, and as in* Macbeth *this action is self-destructive.*
This woodcut shows the title illustration of Marlowe's play in the 1636 edition. Faust is standing in the magic circle, and Mephistopholis appears as the poodle.

Shakespeare, unlike Poe and gothic novelists, does not portray evil in some vague, mysterious and seductive way but in specific, concrete and repellent terms, as when Lady Macbeth visualizes the knocking out of her child's brains or Macbeth looks with revulsion on his bloody hands. Shakespeare is able to do so because he has a very full and precise understanding of it morally and theologically. Evil in Macbeth consists of the disruption of the instinctive and necessary allegiances which hold society together. It manifests itself in the violation of the bonds which link parent with child, ruler with subject, husband with wife. It is, in the literal sense of the word, 'unnatural' or contrary to nature. Hence, in calling up the spirits of night, Lady Macbeth invites them to transform her milk into poison, and, in response to Duncan's murder, his horses 'turn wild in nature', 'contending 'gainst obedience' and devour each other.

The opening chapter of the book of Genesis describes how God created order out of chaos by separating the night from the day, the land from the waters and the fowls of the air from the fishes of the sea, but it is in the nature of evil, as portrayed in *Macbeth*, to demolish this order.

26 **Poe** Edgar Allen Poe, American short story writer and poet (1809–1849)
26 **gothic novelists** writers of novels characterized by mystery, horror and the supernatural
27 **seductive** very desirable or attractive
28 **repellent** causing strong dislike
30 **revulsion** [rɪ'vʌlʃn] strong feeling of disgust
34 **disruption** extreme disturbance
35 **allegiance** [ə'li:dʒəns] loyalty, sense of responsibility and belonging
35 **to manifest itself** to appear
36 **violation** *here:* destruction
36 **bond** s.th. that unites two or more people or groups
38 **literal** basic, true
38 **contrary** ['---] in opposition
42 **to contend** [-'-] to act in opposition
43 **to devour** [dɪ'vaʊə] to eat hungrily
49 **to demolish** to destroy

From New Prefaces to Shakespeare's Plays *by John Wilders, London: Basil Blackwell, 1988, pp. 215–216.*

A closer look

1. How is evil portrayed in *Macbeth*?
2. What 'instinctive and necessary allegiances ...hold society together', according to this text?
3. How does the first chapter of the Bible portray creation (see last paragraph)?
4. In what way are Macbeth's deeds 'unnatural'?

A step further

Can you think of any films or novels in which evil is shown as a concrete image like the witches?

7 Shakespeare Today

Shakespeare is alive and well. Performances of his plays take place all over the world in many languages – and they look different each time. Before you begin this section, discuss any versions of Shakespeare you and your fellow-students may have seen: on stage, on television or at the cinema. Describe the performances and say what you thought of them.

1. Why Shakespeare?

In his novel Babbit, *Sinclair Lewis portrays the Middle America of the 1920s. Chapters 1–7 describe one typical, eventless day in the life of George F. Babbit. Our extract is from chapter 6.*

In the living-room, in the corner of the davenport, Ted settled down to his Home Study; plain geometry, Cicero, and the agonizing metaphors of Comus.

"I don't see why they give us this old-fashioned junk by Milton and Shakespeare and Wordsworth and all these has-beens," he protested. "Oh, I guess I could stand it to see a show by Shakespeare, if they had swell scenery and put on a lot of dog, but to sit down in cold blood and read'em – These teachers - how do they get that way?"

Mrs. Babbit, darning socks, speculated, "Yes, I wonder why. Of course I don't want to fly in the face of the professors and everybody but I do think there's things in Shakespeare - not that I read him much, but when I was young the girls used to show me passages that weren't, really, they weren't at all nice."

Babbit looked up irritably from the comic strips in the Evening Advocate. They composed his favorite literature and art, these illustrated chronicles in which Mr. Mutt hit Mr. Jeff with a rotten egg, and Mother corrected Father's vulgarism by means of a rolling-pin. With the solemn face of a devotee, breathing heavily through his open mouth, he plodded nightly through every picture, and during the rite he detested interruptions. Furthermore, he felt that on the subject of Shakespeare he wasn't really an authority. Neither the *Advocate-Times*, the *Evening Advocate*, nor the *Bulletin of the Zenith Chamber of Commerce* had ever had an editorial on the matter, and until one of them had spoken he found it hard to form an original opinion. But even at risk of floundering in strange bogs, he could not keep out of an open controversy.

"I'll tell you why you have to study Shakespeare and those. It's because they're required for college entrance, and that's all there is to it! Personally, I don't see myself why they stuck'em into an up-to-date high-school system like we have in this state. Be a good deal better if you took Business English, and

1 **davenport** [æ] *(AE)* sofa
3 **agonizing** *here:* very difficult
3 **Comus** play by John Milton (1634)
5 **junk** *(informal)* rubbish, trash
6 **has-been** *(informal)* s.o. who was once important or popular but is no longer so
8 **swell** *(AE, informal)* very good
8 **dog** *here (AE, informal):* showy performance
10 **to get that way** to become like that
11 **to darn** to sew up holes
12 **to fly in the face of s.o.** to go against what s.o. says
19 **chronicle** chronological account
20 **rotten** *here:* no longer good to eat
21 **rolling-pin** cylindrical piece of wood for spreading out dough before baking
22 **solemn** ['sɒləm] very serious
22 **devotee** [ˌdevəʊ'tiː] person who strongly supports and follows s.o.
23 **to plod** to work slowly but steadily
24 **to detest** to dislike intensely
25 **interruption** s.th. that breaks the continuity of a text
28 **Zenith** ['zenɪθ] imaginary town in the American Midwest, setting of *Babbit*
28 **chamber of commerce** group of business people who try to improve conditions for business in their town or city
31 **to flounder** to struggle awkwardly as in deep mud
32 **bog** wet, spongy ground; swamp

learned how to write an ad, or letters that would pull. But there it is, and there's no talk, argument, or discussion about it!"

From Babbit *by Sinclair Lewis, New York: Harcourt Brace Jovanovich, 1922.*

39 **to pull** *here:* to be successful

A closer look

1. Summarize what Ted, Mrs Babbitt and Mr Babbitt have to say about reading Shakespeare at school.
2. Do you think the author agrees with any of his characters? If so, which? Give examples.

In your opinion

3. What do you think: should Shakespeare still be taught at school? Discuss.

2. Is Shakespeare's Shakespeare *our* Shakespeare?

Shakespeare is performed today in theatres all around the world. But how can a theatre director make the plays relevant for our time? Do you think it is legitimate (or even necessary) to change the original text for a modern audience? Should the actresses and actors wear historical costumes or modern dress? In the following text a well-known Shakespeare director reflects on this question.

Mel Gibson as Hamlet (film version)

Kenneth Branagh as Hamlet (stage version 1993)

We cannot know precisely what Shakespeare's Shakespeare was, and if we did, it would not speak to us. Mozart's Mozart is not Karajan's Mozart, produced for our hi-fi age. Yet they are both Mozart. All ages look at the same old-master paintings, but they all see something different. If we could see a Globe production, with Burbage at his best, I am perfectly sure we should not understand it. Its meaning would not be communicated. The art of the theatre is essentially ephemeral, relying on a synthesis of the writers', actors', and audiences' responses. Now, only the texts of Shakespeare's plays remain, and although they are evidence of man's highest genius, it is often difficult for them to yield their meaning because the dialogue between the author and his original audience has long been silenced. We are not Elizabethans. All we can do, by diligent scholarship and hard work, is to try to express Shakespeare's intentions in terms that modern audiences understand. [...]

Interpretation is not a sin, but a necessity because accretions of time have to be stripped away. Most of the stage traditions now surrounding the works are Victorian, none is Elizabethan - Puritans saw to that.

Shakespeare is a 'Classic' and writes of kings and gentlemen as well as commoners. People at once begin to expect abstractions: King Lear is an archetypal gnarled oak, rather than an impossible old man; ancient Romans are supposed to be consistently noble, and the irony that these honourable men commit a political murder is therefore lost. Most of us have a Hollywood view of the past as something grand, wholesome and larger-than-life-size. If our great-great-grandmother had a lover, it is somehow elegant. If our auntie has a lover, it's disgraceful. It's this capacity for ennobling the past that makes most people see Hamlet as a chaste classic, rather than a basic plot so loaded with sex and violence that it demands an 'X' certificate.

Without a return to this human reality, Shakespeare's cunning mixture of a highly wrought text with the naturalistic details of Lear's button or Cleopatra's corset cannot work. And it is out of this mixture of kings and clowns, limpid rhetoric and sudden slang, that his greatest effects are produced.

From "Shakespeare and the Modern Director" by Peter Hall, in: Royal Shakespeare Company 1960–1963, *London: Max Reinhardt Ltd, 1964.*

3 **Karajan** Herbert von Karajan (1908–1989), famous conductor
7 **Burbage** ['bɜːbɪdʒ] Richard Burbage (1567–1619) principal actor of Shakespeare's company, who played all of Shakespeare's major tragic roles
10 **ephemeral** [ɪ'femərəl] lasting only for a short time
14 **to yield** *here:* to convey, to communicate
17 **diligent** ['dɪlɪdʒənt] careful, precise
17 **scholarship** *here:* study
21 **accretion** [æ'kriːʃn] s.th. added
23 **Victorian** from the time of Queen Victoria's reign (1837–1901)
23 **to see to s.th.** to make sure s.th. happens
25 **commoners** ordinary people
26 **archetypal** ['ɑːkɪˌtaɪpəl] of a characteristic type
27 **gnarled** ['nɑːld] twisted and rough from age
27 **oak** large tree found in European forests, with hard, strong wood – *here:* strong old man, to be respected
28 **consistently** [-'---] all the time
32 **wholesome** ['həʊlsəm] *here:* morally upright
34 **disgraceful** shameful, causing dishonour
36 **chaste** morally pure
38 **'X' certificate** official rating of a film which is for adults only
40 **cunning** clever at getting what one wants
40 **wrought** *here:* carefully crafted
43 **limpid** clear, easy to understand

A closer look

1. Explain the following statements:
   a) "We cannot know precisely what Shakespeare's Shakespeare was ..."
   b) "Mozart's Mozart is not Karajan's Mozart produced for our hi-fi age."
2. What do you think Hall means by "a return to this human reality"?

3. What do you think is gained, and what lost, if Shakespeare's plays are 'modernized', e.g. performed in modern dress and in prose versions?

A step further
According to this author, Shakespeare is very "near to us", but he is also "often far away". In the passages by Shakespeare that you have read so far, try to find examples of both: of Shakespeare's closeness to your own experience, and of his belonging to another era.

Sophie Thompson as Rosalind and Jerome Flynn as Orlando in As You Like It *(Royal Shakespeare Company, 1989).*
What are the advantages of producing Shakespeare in modern dress?

3. Shakespeare on the small screen

Between 1978 and 1985 the British Broadcasting Corporation (BBC) produced the complete dramatic works of Shakespeare for television. John Wilders was the literary consultant for this project. In his essay Shakespeare on the Small Screen *he deals with the the positive and negative aspects of creating TV versions of Shakespeare's plays. In the following extract from his essay he talks about the positive aspects.*

Television can restore to Shakespeare's plays the unbroken flow and continuity they almost certainly achieved in the Renaissance theatre. By the simple process of cutting, the director can shift from one scene to another even more swiftly than was possible in Shakespeare's time, when the actors had at least to walk between the stage doors and the acting area. For this reason we have tended to cut those bits of dialogue designed simply to cover entrances and exits. Television performances can also be taken at a more rapid pace than is possible even in the most intimate of modern theatres. In the theatre the actor must ensure that his words, gestures, and the expression of his face are transmitted to many people, some placed at a considerable distance away, and he must therefore adopt a less than natural pace both of speaking and physical expression. But a television actor, placed only a yard or two away from every member of his audience, can speak at a

pace speed

conversational rate and by the merest twitch of an eyebrow convey feeling. Not only does this speed of performance give to the plays a tighter unity, but it probably restores to them the pace and rhythm they achieved when they were first produced. The Globe Theatre, polygonal in shape, built largely of wood, rubble, and plaster, unencumbered by the sound-absorbing materials of carpeting and upholstery, was, I imagine, an acoustically lively place. The actor, in close proximity to his audience, could have rattled off his lines at a rate which made the "two hours' traffic of our stage" a fairly accurate description. Television can also do justice to the way in which the plays are constructed. Shakespeare takes care to keep his audience continually surprised and refreshed by alternating between dialogue and soliloquy, episodes in which the stage is crowded and others where it is occupied by few, or only one character. These correspond in television terms to long shots and close-ups. It is as though the dramatist were signalling from his grave to the director and telling him focus his lens. Both directly and indirectly Shakespeare has profoundly influenced the language of film and television.

From "Shakespeare and the Small Screen" by John Wilders, in: Deutsche Shakespeare Gesellschaft West, Jahrbuch 1982, *Bochum: Verlag Ferdinand Kamp, 1982, pp. 61–62.*

19 **mere** *here:* slight
19 **twitch** short, sudden repeated movement of a muscle
25 **rubble** pieces of bricks etc. remaining after a building has been demolished
25 **plaster** smooth, white covering on walls
25 **unencumbered** not burdened
26 **to absorb** to take s.th. in so that it is no longer noticeable
26 **upholstery** cloth covering on chairs etc.
28 **proximity** nearness
28 **to rattle off (lines)** to deliver lines quickly
34 **soliloquy** [sə'lɪləkwɪ] speech made by an actor to himself/herself and the audience and not to others in the play
36 **to correspond to** to parallel
37 **long shot** *here:* view from a distance
39 **lens** thin, curved piece of glass in a camera
40 **profoundly** very deeply

A closer look

1. How can television "restore the original unbroken flow" of a Shakespearean play?
2. a) What methods did Shakespeare use to introduce variety into his plays?
   b) How can a television production do justice to the construction of a Shakespearean play?

A step further

1. Look at the still from *Romeo and Juliet.* What features does it contain that show it is a film and not a stage production?
2. Borrow a BBC film of a Shakespeare play from a British Council office or a commercial videotheque if none is available at your school. Watch the film and write down your impressions. Then talk about the film in class.

Romeo pays a rather unorthodox visit to Juliet – from a BBC-TV production of Romeo and Juliet.

4. Shakespeare in Stratford-upon-Avon

Shakespeare's home town of Stratford attracts more tourists from all over the world than any other town in England except London. But how does this affect Stratford?

Although Stratford-upon-Avon remains a small market town closely linked with the Warwickshire countryside, it has now become a gathering-place of all nations. This has been brought about by a remarkable growth of the international appreciation of Shakespeare, due in part to improved communications and publicity, but largely to the development of education, in which the teaching of English and the study of Shakespeare's plays have played an important part.

Whereas a century ago visitors to Shakespeare's Birthplace numbered barely 6,000 a year, the annual total is now over half a million. More than half of these come from overseas and represent at least a hundred different nationalities.

From The Shakespeare Book *by Levi Fox, Norwich: Jarrold and Sons Limited (in association with the Shakespeare Birthplace Trust). Levi Fox is a former director of the Shakespeare Birthplace Trust.*

Now listen to what two former artistic directors of the Royal Shakespeare Company in Stratford, Terry Hands and Peter Hall, and the present artistic director, Adrian Noble, have to say on the subject (in an interview with Michael Coveney):

COVENEY: We are now in 'Shakespeare Country', according to the road signs. The is a McDonald's along Waterside, next door to 'The Wonderful World of Shakespeare' and there are many more day trippers. Is it becoming an Elizabethan theme park?

HALL: The place used to be a rather cool, restrained little market town that hated the theatre and the actors and thought we were making some sort of immoral living off their backs. In a way that was honest and an example of typically British Philistinism and I rather enjoyed it. What I don't enjoy now is that the place is polluted by very cheap tourism.

HANDS: But surely it has to be that way, inevitable in the growth of the theatre. It's like the old cathedrals, which were always surrounded by a *souk* or a bazaar.

ADRIAN NOBLE: [...] The commercialisation I'm not so keen on, but the place is increasingly becoming a centre of Shakespearean studies. Young people come here from all over the world in the summer. I love walking round the streets and hearing a great variety of languages.

3 **Waterside** street on which the Royal Shakespeare Theatre is located
3 **The Wonderful World of Shakespeare** multi-media presentation about Shakespeare and his world
4 **day-tripper** s.o. who goes to a place of interest for one day
5 **theme park** place which has attractions and amusements focused upon a particular theme or character
6 **restrained** calm and unemotional
10 **Philistinism** attitude of not liking or caring about the arts
13 **inevitable** certain to happen, not to be avoided
15 **souk** [sʊk] *(Arabic)* Arab market where all sorts of goods are sold

From The Observer, *28 June, 1992.*

A closer look

1. What reasons does Levi Fox give for the growth in the appreciation of Shakespeare over the last 100 years?

2. a) What do you think Hall means by saying that Stratford is "polluted by very cheap tourism"?
   b) Compare Hands' reply with what you know about the theatre in Shakespeare's day.
3. What does Noble find particularly attractive about Stratford?

A step further
Visit Stratford-upon-Avon one day. Go there preferably in spring and outside the holiday season.

A street scene in Stratford-upon-Avon

5. The mysterious figure on the bank-card

Not only are Shakespeare's plays transported into a modern setting – they are also transported around the globe and translated into other languages.

I take out my bank-card. In the bottom right-hand corner is a picture of Shakespeare overprinted with the words "Cheque guarantee". But hold the card up to the light and something strange happens. The colour, form and angle of Shakespeare's face alters: in profile he seems to be a beaming Bard, head-on he is a sombre sage. The picture is a kitsch symbol of a basic truth.

Shakespeare stands for order, security, reliability. At the same time, he is shifting, elusive, infinitely variable. It is a duality which lies at the heart of the modern Shakespeare industry.

For politicians he is constantly a handy source of quotation: on the day of the Gulf ceasefire, Sir Julian Amery remarked of Saddam Hussein, "We have scotched the snake, not killed it" (apparently forgetting these words are spoken by, and not about, Macbeth). For business enterprises, Shakespeare is a potent commercial weapon. In a recent Stratford programme, British Telecom had an advert telling us that "Poor communication was the death of those star-crossed lovers, Romeo and Juliet. While the speed and clarity of today's communications might well have saved them." Though, personally, I wouldn't bank on it.

3 **cheque guarantee** [tʃek] *when the owner of a card pays by cheque, the card shows that the cheque is legal*
5 **to alter** ['ɔ:ltə] to change
6 **to beam** to smile broadly
6 **Bard** *here:* name for Shakespeare (*usually:* poet)
6 **sombre** ['sɒmbə] serious
6 **sage** wise person
8 **reliability** [-ˌ--'---] dependability
9 **elusive** hard to find or grasp
9 **infinitely** ['----] without end
12 **handy** very useful
13 **Gulf** *here:* war following Iraq's invasion of Kuwait in 1990
13 **ceasefire** end of fighting in a war
14 **to scotch** *(old use)* to burn (skin)
20 **star-crossed** plagued by bad luck
23 **(not) to bank on s.th.** (not) to depend on s.th., believing it to be true *(usually negative)*

So, on the one hand, we have the Stratford lad as symbol of national pride and quality goods [...]

But, on the other hand, there is the infinitely more mysterious Shakespeare: the dramatist of no fixed abode whose work takes on new resonances in different cultures. In Europe he seems European: in Asia, Asian. And of his booming popularity, there is no doubt. The sold-out productions in Paris this spring have been Peter Zadek's *Mesure pour Mesure* and Peter Brook's *La Tempête*. In Hamburg on a recent Sunday night I found there was a choice at the two major theatres between Jurgen Flimm's *Was Ihr Wollt* (Twelfth Night) and Michael Bogdanov's *Romeo and Julia*. No wonder the Germans call him "unser Shakespeare". [...]

27 **no fixed abode** no permanent address
30 **booming** growing very fast

A scene from Russian director Michael Tumanishvili's production of A Midsummer Night's Dream, *performed by the Georgian Film Actors's Studio of Tbilisi (Georgia) in The Pit (Edinburgh), November 1994.*

A closer look

1. What duality does the bank card stand for?
2. Which two approaches to Shakespeare's "multi-dimensionality" does Billington describe?

My belief is that, in practice, there are two basic modern approaches to Shakespeare's multi-dimensionality. One is to anchor the plays in local experience in order to achieve universality: a classic example is Richard Eyre's *Richard III* which was filled with English iconography (khaki soldiery, Edwardian banquets, sun-dappled pastoral backcloths) but which reportedly achieved immediate resonance in East European countries. The other approach, adopted by Peter Brook in *La Tempête*, is to bring together actors of different colours, races and backgrounds and exploit their individuality: in Britain today, given the diversity of our society, we have a golden opportunity to attempt a multi-racial Shakespeare which still largely goes begging.

We cannot help but see Shakespeare in terms of our own language, history and culture; but we need urgently to widen that definition of culture not by doing ludicrous, down-market pop travesties of the plays but by working towards racially integrated productions. Only then will we begin to reach the heart of the mysteriously shifting and elusive figure on the bank-card.

39 **approach** way of looking at s.th.
40 **to anchor** to give a firm base to
43 **iconography** set of symbols with well-known meanings
43 **Edwardian** relating to the style of art and dress etc. popular in England at the time of the reign of King Edward VII (1841–1910)
44 **pastoral** showing scenes of country life
44 **backcloth** large piece of cloth at the back of a stage, painted
48 **to exploit** *here:* to make use of
52 **to go begging** to be unwanted or unused
56 **ludicrous** absurd to the point of provoking laughter
56 **down-market** of poor quality, cheap
56 **travesty** parody that spoils the quality of s.th.

By Michael Billington, in The Guardian Weekly, *May 5, 1991.*